PROTECTION

The Power of the 91st Psalm

GLORIA COPELAND

KENNETH COPELAND
PUBLICATIONS

Unless otherwise noted, all scripture is from the *King James Version* of the Bible.

Scripture quotations marked *Amplified Bible, Classic Edition* are from the *Amplified® Bible,* © 1954, 1958, 1962, 1964, 1965, 1987 by The Lockman Foundation. Used by permission.

Your Promise of Protection
The Power of the 91st Psalm

ISBN-10 1-57562-715-9   30-0546
ISBN-13 978-1-57562-715-1

27 26 25 24 23 22   12 11 10 9 8 7

Kenneth Copeland Publications
Fort Worth, TX 76192-0001

For more information about Kenneth Copeland Ministries, visit kcm.org or call 1-800-600-7395 (U.S. only) or +1-817-852-6000.

CONTENTS

PSALM NINETY-ONE
King James Version

¹ He that dwelleth in the secret place of the most High shall abide under the shadow of the Almighty.

² I will say of the Lord, He is my refuge and my fortress: my God; in him will I trust.

³ Surely he shall deliver thee from the snare of the fowler, and from the noisome pestilence.

⁴ He shall cover thee with his feathers, and under his wings shalt thou trust: his truth shall be thy shield and buckler.

⁵ Thou shall not be afraid for the terror by night; nor for the arrow that flieth by day;

⁶ nor for the pestilence that walketh in darkness; nor for the destruction that wasteth at noonday.

⁷ A thousand shall fall at thy side, and ten thousand at thy right hand; but it shall not come nigh thee.

⁸ Only with thine eyes shalt thou behold and see the reward of the wicked.

⁹ Because thou hast made the Lord, which is my refuge, even the most High, thy habitation;

¹⁰ there shall no evil befall thee, neither shall any plague come nigh thy dwelling.

¹¹ For he shall give his angels charge over thee, to keep thee in all thy ways.

¹² They shall bear thee up in their hands, lest thou dash thy foot against a stone.

¹³ Thou shalt tread upon the lion and adder: the young lion and the dragon shalt thou trample under feet.

¹⁴ Because he hath set his love upon me, therefore will I deliver him: I will set him on high, because he hath known my name.

¹⁵ He shall call upon me, and I will answer him: I will be with him in trouble; I will deliver him, and honour him.

¹⁶ With long life will I satisfy him, and show him my salvation.

PSALM NINETY-ONE
Amplified Bible, Classic Edition

¹ He who dwells in the secret place of the Most High shall remain stable and fixed under the shadow of the Almighty [Whose power no foe can withstand].

² I will say of the Lord, He is my Refuge and my Fortress, my God; on Him I lean and rely, and in Him I [confidently] trust!

³ For [then] He will deliver you from the snare of the fowler and from the deadly pestilence.

⁴ [Then] He will cover you with His pinions, and under His wings shall you trust and find refuge; His truth and His faithfulness are a shield and a buckler.

⁵ You shall not be afraid of the terror of the night, nor of the arrow (the evil plots and slanders of the wicked) that flies by day,

⁶ Nor of the pestilence that stalks in darkness, nor of the destruction and sudden death that surprise and lay waste at noonday.

⁷ A thousand may fall at your side, and ten thousand at your right hand, but it shall not come near you.

⁸ Only a spectator shall you be [yourself inaccessible in the secret place of the Most High] as you witness the reward of the wicked.

⁹ Because you have made the Lord your refuge, and the Most High your dwelling place,

¹⁰ There shall no evil befall you, nor any plague or calamity come near your tent.

¹¹ For He will give His angels [especial] charge over you, to accompany and defend and preserve you in all your ways [of obedience and service].

¹² They shall bear you up on their hands, lest you dash your foot against a stone.

¹³ You shall tread upon the lion and adder; the young lion and the serpent shall you trample under foot.

¹⁴ Because he has set his love upon Me, therefore will I deliver him; I will set him on high, because he knows and understands My name [has a personal

knowledge of My mercy, love, and kindness—trusts and relies on Me, knowing I will never forsake him, no, never].

¹⁵ He shall call upon Me, and I will answer him; I will be with him in trouble, I will deliver him and honor him.

¹⁶ With long life will I satisfy him and show him My salvation.

CHAPTER 1

WHAT ARE WE GOING TO DO?

"God said to Noah...make yourself an ark."
(Genesis 6:13-14, *AMPC*)

With all the violence and calamity bearing down on us these days, that's a question we hear a lot. What are we going to do about crime in our streets? What are we going to do about economic failures? What are we going to do about international problems?

I'll tell you what we'd *better* do. We'd better take a lesson from Noah. Look in Genesis 6 at the Bible's description of the earth back in his day and you'll see why I say that.

The earth was depraved and putrid in

God's sight, and the land was filled with violence (desecration, infringement, outrage, assault, and lust for power). And God looked upon the world and saw how degenerate, debased, and vicious it was, for all humanity had corrupted their way upon the earth and lost their true direction (verses 11-12, *AMPC*).

With a few exceptions that verse sounds like a description of today's world, doesn't it?

What did God tell Noah to do about this desperate situation? He said, "Noah, make yourself an ark." That ark was to provide Noah's deliverance from the destruction to come. It was to keep him safe when the whole world was perishing around him.

START BUILDING

I believe God is saying to us today, just like He did to Noah, "Build yourself an ark."

Not an ark made of wood, but an ark made of the Word of God.

Do you realize that what you know from the Word of God will save your life? That's right. If you build God's promises of protection and deliverance into your heart and life, you can live in this crazy world with all its danger and still feel secure. You don't have to be frightened by the things that are happening around you because even in the worst of times, God has proven He has the wonderful ability to deliver His people from danger.

Notice I said *His people.* Today, as in Noah's day, there are two groups of people on the earth: God's people and the rest of the world. There is the family of Satan and the family of God.

Because God has already provided the gift of salvation to all men, the people in the world group have the option to change groups at any time by accepting Jesus as Savior. John 3:16 says, "For God so loved the world, that he gave his only begotten Son, that whosoever believeth in him should not perish, but have everlasting life." But until they accept Him, the world group won't enjoy the benefits God's people have.

As a result, the lives of these two groups can be strikingly different. They may be living in the same city—even the same family. Yet one of them has a covenant with God and the other doesn't. One group will live in safety while the other is subjected to the dangers of the world on their own.

"It shall be well with him [the righteous]..." but "Woe unto the wicked! it shall be ill with him..." (Isaiah 3:10-11). You may hear someone prophesy about how bad things are going to become on the earth. Then you may hear someone else prophesy about the power and blessings that lie ahead of us. Both prophecies may be accurate. But the first is speaking to the people of the world and the second is speaking to the people of God.

Noah was a wonderful example of just how

capable God is of protecting His people in the midst of a corrupt and crumbling civilization. The whole world went down around him, but the eight people in his family remained perfectly safe.

Some people say, "Oh yes, I know I am eternally safe. I know that because I am born again, I'll go to heaven when I die."

But I'm not just talking about heavenly security. I am telling you that you can have physical security, financial security and every other kind of security you need to live in victory right here on this earth.

LOADED WITH BENEFITS!

You see, salvation includes more than just the guarantee of going to heaven in the sweet by-and-by. That's just the beginning. *Salvation* is a big word. In the Greek language it literally means deliverance, safety, preservation, material and temporal deliverance from danger and apprehension, pardon, restoration, healing, wholeness and soundness.

If I were to use just one word, I would say salvation is soundness in every area of life. It includes healing for your body, peace for your mind, righteousness for your spirit, physical and spiritual protection, prosperity and financial blessing.

I like what Psalm 68:19-20 says: "Blessed be the Lord, Who bears our burdens and carries us day by day, even the God Who is our salvation! ...God is to us a God of deliverances and salvation; and to God the Lord belongs escape from death [setting us free]" *(AMPC)*.

That same scripture in the *King James Version* says, "Blessed be the Lord, who daily loadeth us with benefits, even the God of our salvation...." Just think about that. Every day God loads us with the benefits of salvation! He loads us with forgiveness, healing, safety, security, prosperity and deliverance from danger.

IT'S NOT AUTOMATIC

Now you may be wondering, *If safety and security and healing and deliverance are all part of my salvation, why haven't I been experiencing all these things?*

Because they don't come automatically. They are manifest in your life only as you begin to trust God for them specifically.

Let me explain. Remember when you were born again? You discovered God's Word promised if you would repent and confess Jesus as your Lord, you would be forgiven of your sins and translated from the kingdom of darkness into the kingdom of God's Son (Colossians 1:13). So you believed, obeyed, accepted Jesus as Savior and you were instantly saved. But that didn't heal you from the flu, did it?

No, before you could be healed from the flu, you had to hear God's Word about your healing. You had to learn that Jesus bore your sicknesses and carried your diseases. Until you began to believe for healing—until you trusted God for it specifically and stood in faith for it—you didn't walk in divine health.

The same is true about anything. Until you find out what actually belongs to you through the blood of Jesus, you can't lay hold of it by faith and see it happen in your life. That's why it's so important to know God's promises of protection. You receive blessings by faith—and faith comes by hearing the Word. You can't have faith for something you don't know about.

If someone were to deposit a million dollars in an account with your name on it but didn't bother to tell you about it, you'd never be able to enjoy it, would you? The money would belong to you, but you wouldn't know to withdraw it. So it would sit in the bank unused. That's the sad situation so many believers are in today when it comes to the mighty benefits of salvation through Jesus the Anointed One.

CHAPTER 2

KEEPING THE CONDITIONS

"He Who dwells in the secret place of the Most High shall remain stable and fixed under the shadow of the Almighty [Whose power no foe can withstand]."

(Psalm 91:1, *AMPC*)

Once you know from God's Word that divine protection belongs to you, there are conditions you must keep to activate that protection in your life. The Word of God makes these conditions very clear.

You can find the first one at the beginning of Psalm 91: "He who abides in the secret place of the Most High shall remain fixed under the shadow of the Almighty."

If you are to enjoy God's protection, you're going to have to abide in Him. To *abide* means "to dwell in." It is a word that implies a permanent dwelling place, not a temporary situation. It is the place where you make your home. This word doesn't indicate a coming in and going out but a continual dwelling under God's shadow.

What does it take to become an abider? It takes putting God's Word in your heart, for one thing. In John 15:7, Jesus said, "If you live in Me [abide vitally united to Me] and My words remain in you and continue to live in your hearts, ask whatever you will, and it shall be done for you" *(AMPC).*

The truth that is alive in your heart is the truth you act on every day. It doesn't come from simply reading a scripture once, shouting hallelujah and going on. It comes from knowing the Word so well that it comes to your thinking instantly in a crisis situation. Truth comes alive in you when you think about it, meditate on it and apply it to your life. At the very moment of danger, the Word of God is your first thought.

Abiding under the shadow of the Almighty is the result of spending so much time in the Word of God and in His presence that His truth governs your actions without even a conscious thought. If you want to be an abider, you can't afford to simply get into the Word for a while and then quit. You need to be consistent. Stay in the Word day after day after day. Take the 91st Psalm into yourself daily until it becomes engrafted in your heart.

Remember this: It's the Word you act on today that will get you delivered. It's not what you heard last year. It isn't even what you know. It's what you do. Keep yourself full of God's Word and you will do it.

If that sounds like a tall order to you, let me promise you something. For every minute you invest in the Word of God, you'll get back a hundredfold in health, faith and deliverance. You'll never regret a second of it.

DISOBEDIENCE IS DANGEROUS

Another definition of abiding is simply obeying. First John 3:6 says, "Whosoever abideth in him sinneth not." The reverse of that is also true—whoever sins (or is disobedient) does not abide in Him.

If you'll look at the first chapter of Proverbs, you'll see just how dangerous disobedience can be. You will see why, when most people need supernatural protection, it isn't there for them.

Beginning in verse 23, God says:

If you will turn (repent) and give heed to my reproof, behold, I [Wisdom] will pour out my spirit upon you, I will make my words known to you. Because I have called and you refused [to answer], have stretched out my hand and no man heeded it, and you treated as nothing all my counsel and would accept none of my reproof, I also will laugh at your calamity; I will mock when the thing comes that shall cause you terror and panic.... Then will they call upon me [Wisdom] but I will not answer; they will seek me early and diligently but they will not find me. Because they hated knowledge and did not choose the reverent and worshipful fear of the Lord.... But whoso hearkens to me [Wisdom] shall dwell securely and in confident trust and shall be quiet, without fear or dread of evil (verses 23-26, 28-29, 33, *AMPC*).

Thank God, we're living in the day of grace and mercy and it's never too late to call upon the Lord. But if you haven't been abiding in the Word (God's wisdom revealed to us), it's going to be difficult for you to call on Him in faith when calamity comes. If you've been living every day by the world's standards, at the moment of crisis it will be hard to take your dependence off the world and put it on Him.

So you need to start abiding in the Word of God now! If you don't it will eventually cost you more than you want to pay.

Proverbs 1:29-31 says, "Because they hated knowledge and did not choose the reverent and worshipful fear of the Lord, would accept none of my counsel, and despised all my reproof, therefore shall they eat of the fruit of their own way and be satiated with their own devices" *(AMPC)*.

In other words, if you're going to live like the world, your outcome is going to be like that of the world. "But whoso hearkens to me [Wisdom] shall dwell securely and in confident trust and shall be quiet, without fear or dread of evil" (Proverbs 1:33, *AMPC)*. Now that's the kind of supernatural protection promised to those who abide.

CHAPTER 3

SAY SOMETHING!

"I will say of the Lord, He is my Refuge and my Fortress, my God; on Him I lean and rely, and in Him I [confidently] trust!"

(Psalm 91:2, *AMPC*)

I will say! There's something else important about the person who lives in the protective shadow of the Almighty. He speaks in faith. He says of the Lord, "He is my Refuge and my Fortress; my God; on Him I lean and rely, and in Him I [confidently] trust!"

This man is doing more than just trusting God with his heart, he's saying it with his mouth! That's what you need to be doing too. You see, faith brings God's supernatural power into this natural realm. And faith is released into this natural realm by words. So you need to be saying, "God is my refuge. He is my fortress. I trust in Him!"

I can't count the times I've said those words. I've meditated on the 91st Psalm and said it so often that at any moment of danger, that is what springs up inside me. When I run into trouble, my mouth doesn't say, "I'm scared to death." My mouth says, "The Lord is my refuge. He shall deliver me!"

Make up your mind right now to get your mouth in line with God's Word. Do you know what will happen if you do? You'll be able to go to sleep at night. You won't lie there in worry or fear. Instead, you'll trust God with every part of your life. And no matter what circumstance you're in, you'll be able to just turn over and go to sleep. The Bible says God gives His beloved sleep (Psalm 127:2).

One night, years ago, Ken and I were spending the night in an Israeli kibbutz. It was located very close to the border where enemy raids were frequent—and often deadly. I had thoughts that we might be in danger.

So what did I do? I said of the Lord out loud, "He is my refuge and my fortress. I trust Him with my life." Then I turned over and went to sleep.

You can do the same thing. If you'll meditate on this verse long enough and speak it out often enough you'll be able to go right to sleep wherever you are. You can sleep by faith!

CHAPTER 4

THE FOWLER'S SNARE

"For [then] He will deliver you from the snare of the fowler and from the deadly pestilence. [Then] He will cover you with His pinions, and under His wings shall you trust and find refuge; His truth and His faithfulness are a shield and a buckler."

(Psalm 91:3-4, *AMPC*)

When you "say" until you have that kind of peace on the inside, you can be assured you'll have supernatural protection on the outside. You can be sure God will "deliver you from the snare of the fowler and from the noisome pestilence" (Psalm 91:3).

What's the "snare of the fowler"? The traps laid by the devil to cause you harm. (One friend of ours says the devil is the fowler because he comes along and tries to foul things up!) And the *Amplified Bible, Classic Edition* defines *pestilence* as "...plagues; malignant and contagious or infectious epidemic diseases which are deadly and devastating" (Luke 21:11). Doesn't that sound like AIDS or cancer?

I like the 91st Psalm because it's always so up-to-date. No matter what kind of new threats the devil comes up with, the 91st Psalm promises deliverance from them. Epidemic diseases, nuclear weapons, chemical warfare—read Psalm 91 closely and you'll see it covers every one of them.

CHAPTER 5

SURROUNDED BY DANGER

"You shall not be afraid of the terror of the night, nor of the arrow (the evil plots and slanders of the wicked) that flies by day, nor of the pestilence that stalks in darkness, nor of the destruction and sudden death that surprise and lay waste at noonday. A thousand may fall at your side, and ten thousand at your right hand, but it shall not come near you. Only a spectator shall you be [yourself inaccessible in the secret place of the Most High] as you witness the reward of the wicked."

(Psalm 91:5-8, *AMPC*)

We live in a time in which weapons can kill thousands of people at once. Chemical weapons or nuclear warfare can destroy whole cities. But despite the magnitude of the disaster, God has promised we can stand in the midst of it untouched!

Notice I said, in the midst of it! Clearly, when God says "a thousand may fall at your side," He's not talking about heaven. He's talking about a place here on earth where you're seeing some disastrous things happen to the wicked all around you. Yet you are totally protected—covered by an invisible shield. You are in the secret place the world knows nothing about. When you're in that place, it doesn't matter how terrible your situation might be, you can make it through in safety. (See Psalm 5:11-12, 27:5, *AMPC*. Put these scriptures in your mouth!)

Ken and I have a friend who proved that beyond a doubt. He took the 91st Psalm into battle with him when he was in Vietnam years ago. He broke it down verse by verse and applied it to his specific situation.

To him, the arrow that flies by day mentioned in verse 5 meant the bullets of the enemy. So he would say, "I shall not be afraid of the terror of the night nor of the bullets of the enemy." The pestilence that stalks in darkness and the destruction and sudden death that surprise and lay waste at noonday meant the Viet Cong and the deadly booby traps they had set.

And when he read "a thousand may fall at your side, and ten thousand at your right hand, but it shall not come near you," he knew he would be protected even in open combat. So he would agree and say, "I'll only observe these things, I won't be a victim of them."

Do you know he came through that war untouched? He had been in the midst of heavy fighting, in some of the most dangerous places in Vietnam, yet he believed God for his deliverance and walked away unharmed.

How could that happen? Look again at Psalm 91:4: "He will cover you with His pinions, and under His wings shall you trust and find refuge; His truth and His faithfulness are a shield and buckler" *(AMPC)*.

Our friend was hidden from the enemy. God covered him up like a mother eagle covers her babies by spreading her feathers over them. The devil couldn't get to him because God's truth and faithfulness were the shield and buckler that kept the enemy at bay.

CHAPTER 6

DON'T FORGET TO DO YOUR PART

"Because you have made the Lord your refuge, and the Most High your dwelling place, there shall no evil befall you, nor any plague or calamity come near your tent."

(Psalm 91:9-10, *AMPC*)

No doubt, by now you're getting pretty excited about God's protection. But before we go on, I want to remind you once more—receiving that protection is conditional. You have to know what God has said before that shield and buckler will work for you. You have to hear it from God's Word and receive it for yourself saying, "That's mine. Deliverance from God belongs to me!"

Look again at the first part of verse 9: "Because you have made the Lord your refuge, and the Most High your dwelling place." I have that first word, "because," circled in my Bible. This verse tells you how to position yourself in the secret place. It says because you have made the Lord your refuge by obeying verses 1 and 2, you can count on Him to do His part by rescuing you from danger. Notice verse 3 in the *Amplified Bible, Classic Edition* starts "For [then] He will deliver you...."

When you think of Psalm 91, remember: the first two verses are what *we* do and say. Verses 3-15 are God's answer and commitment to us. When we do our part—saying and trusting, God does His part—delivering and preserving.

CHAPTER 7

ANGELS AT YOUR SERVICE

"For He will give His angels [especial] charge over you to accompany and defend and preserve you in all your ways [of obedience and service]. They shall bear you up on their hands, lest you dash your foot against a stone."

(Psalm 91:11-12, *AMPC*)

One of the ways God carries out your deliverance is through angels. You literally have angels at your service. Did you know that? The Bible teaches they are sent to serve you and keep you safe as you carry out God's will in your life. Hebrews 1:14 says, "Are not the angels all ministering spirits (servants) sent out in the service [of God for the assistance] of those who are to inherit salvation?" *(AMPC)*.

The angel of the Lord encamps round about those who fear God, to deliver them (Psalm 34:7). Your angels set up camp wherever you are. When you move, they move. When you go to town, they go to town. When you go to the grocery store, they go to the grocery store. When you go to war, they go to war.

Second Kings 6 gives us a picture of how angels operate. Elisha, the prophet of God, had received inside information from God on the strategy of enemy nations. He'd passed that information along to the king of Israel so Israel was never caught off guard in any military maneuver.

When the enemy king realized information was leaking to Israel he assumed they had a spy in their camp.

"Who is telling the king of Israel our military secrets?" he demanded.

His servant answered, "None of us, my lord

O king. But that prophet Elisha knows what we say in our bed chambers." (See 2 Kings 6:11-12.)

So the enemy king and his entire army took off in pursuit of one man! They surrounded the city where Elisha was staying and "when the servant of the man of God was risen early, and gone forth, behold, an host compassed the city both with horses and chariots" (verse 15).

Elisha's servant panicked. A whole army against the two of them looked like very bad odds. "Master, what are we going to do?" he cried.

"Fear not," Elisha told him, "for they that be with us are more than they that be with them" (verse 16).

Don't you know that servant was counting? One...two! There are two of us and thousands of them. Elisha must be losing his mind. But Elisha wasn't looking at the natural realm. He was seeing into the spirit realm.

Elisha prayed, "Lord, open his eyes that he

may see." Notice he didn't say, "Lord, protect me." He didn't need to ask for protection, he knew it was there.

"And the Lord opened the eyes of the young man; and he saw: and, behold, the mountain was full of horses and chariots of fire round about Elisha" (verse 17). The mountain was full of protection for Elisha! God had sent battalions of angels to protect him. I'm sure the extra angels had arrived before the enemy army ever got there. I say "extra" because we have angels surrounding us all the time and those regulars can quickly be reinforced.

FEAR NOT!

Before we leave this account about Elisha, I want you to pay special attention to the answer he gave his frightened servant in verse 16. "Fear not." Those were the first words Elisha spoke.

What is the very first thing you're to do in trouble? Fear not. If you fear, you open the door to the devil. If you trust God, you open the door to God.

Over and over in the Bible God exhorts us not to fear. Psalms 91:5 begins, "You shall not be afraid..." *(AMPC)*. When angels would appear to people, "Fear not!" were usually the first words out of their mouths. That's because fear and faith don't mix. Fear and faith cannot come out of you at the same time.

When you start saying things that are out of line with the Word of God, when you start speaking in fear instead of in faith, you bind the hands of your angels. You prevent them from doing their job. Psalm 103:20-21 tells us why: "Bless the Lord, ye his angels, that excel in strength, that do his commandments, hearkening unto the voice of his word. Bless ye the Lord, all ye his hosts; ye ministers of his, that do his pleasure."

Angels hearken to the voice of God's Word. They respond to the Word! So when your heart is full of faith and your mouth is saying, "A thousand may fall at my side, ten thousand at my right hand but it will not come near me," they put that Word into action and protect you.

But when your heart is full of fear and your mouth is speaking words of unbelief, your angels can only stand by helplessly. It's not that they abandon you, it's just that they have nothing to act on.

Never, ever underestimate the power of your words. Scripture teaches us that God speaks of things that are not as though they were. (See Romans 4:17.) That's how He creates—He speaks things into existence.

Whether you realize it or not, you do the same thing. When you speak words by faith according to the Word of God, you are opening the door for God's protection and blessing. When you speak words in fear that are contrary to the Word, you are opening the door for the devil to bring you destruction.

I know these are dangerous days. Almost every day on the news we hear about innocent people who are shot just standing on the street corner or sitting in a restaurant. (Flying arrows aren't doing much damage these days, but bullets can be pretty deadly!) But when you have the Word of God alive inside you, you don't have to worry about the unexpected. God is never caught by surprise.

So put away fear. Rebuke it out of your life. Talk to it as if it were a snake. Say, "Fear, in the Name of Jesus, I command you to be gone!" Then put it under your feet. Stomp it out of your life. If it rears its head again, rid yourself of it as swiftly as you would a rattlesnake.

Get your heart established on God's Word and your mouth full of faith. Keep your angels on the job. You never know when you're going to need them!

OUT OF THE FIRE

One of the most exciting scriptural examples of God's angelic delivering power is found in Daniel 3. There we see three of God's people in big trouble with the government. The king of the Babylonian empire had made an image and declared that "Whoso falleth not down and worshippeth, [that image] that he should be cast into the midst of a burning fiery furnace" (verse 11).

Now, these three men of God—Shadrach, Meshach and Abednego—happened to be on the king's own staff. They were Hebrews who had been captured, but God's blessing was on them to such a degree they had been given great responsibility over the affairs of Babylon. They served and trusted God. So despite the king's decree, they refused to bow down to that image.

As we read this story, I want you to notice that these three men fit the pattern of the man described in Psalm 91. They were faithful to

God. They abided in Him. And when they were faced with danger, instead of crying and whining about it, they spoke words of faith.

When the king threatened to throw them into the fiery furnace for refusing to bow down to his idol, they said, "If it be so, our God whom we serve is able to deliver us from the burning fiery furnace, and he will deliver us out of thine hand, O king. But if not, be it known unto thee, O king, that we will not serve thy gods, nor worship the golden image which thou hast set up" (verses 17-18).

In other words, they refused to bow and they refused to be afraid. They said, "Our God is able to deliver us!"

That made the king so angry he had that furnace heated up seven times hotter than usual. The heat was so intense that the guards who threw Shadrach, Meshach and Abednego into the furnace were killed instantly. "And these three men, Shadrach, Meshach, and Abednego, fell down bound into the midst of the burning fiery furnace. Then...the king was astonished, and rose up in haste, and spake, and said unto his counselors, Did not we cast three men bound into the midst of the fire? ...and they have no hurt; and the form of the fourth is like the Son of God (verses 23-25).

Why didn't Shadrach, Meshach and Abednego burn? It certainly wasn't because the fire had no power. It had power all right. It had enough power to kill the mighty men in the king's army who threw them into it. It just had no power over the bodies of God's men. In fact, the Bible tells us not even a "hair of their head (was) singed, neither were their coats changed, nor the smell of fire had passed on them" (verse 27).

What's more, God sent His angel into the fire to watch over them while they were there.

Then Nebuchadnezzar spake, and said, Blessed be the God of Shadrach, Meshach, and Abed-nego, who hath sent his angel, and delivered his servants that trusted in him, and have changed the king's word, and yielded their bodies, that they might not serve nor worship any god, except their own God. Therefore I make a decree, That every people, nation, and language, which speak any thing amiss against the God of Shadrach, Meshach and Abed-nego, shall be cut in pieces, and their houses shall be made a dunghill: because there is no other God that can deliver after this sort. Then the king promoted Shadrach, Meshach, and Abed-nego, in the province of Babylon (verses 28-30).

Isn't that a great testimony of God's delivering power? When Shadrach, Meshach and Abednego's enemies tried to get rid of them, these three servants of God were promoted instead! They made the Lord their refuge. Their trust was in Him. He was their deliverer and they never stopped saying so. They refused to compromise or give in to the intimidation of the enemy. They did not bow and they did not burn!

THE SECRET PLACE

I've always loved the story of Shadrach, Meshach and Abednego. But for years, I wondered exactly how they could come through a fire like that without even smelling like smoke. Then one day I was reading Psalm 27 and I found out: "The Lord is my Light and my Salvation—whom shall I fear or dread? The Lord is the Refuge and Stronghold of my life—of whom shall I be afraid? ...For in the day of trouble He will hide me in His shelter; in the secret place of His tent will He hide me; He will set me high upon a rock" (verses 1, 5, *AMPC*).

When Shadrach, Meshach and Abednego went into that fiery furnace, the presence of God settled upon them like a bubble. It surrounded them. It covered them. They didn't get hot. They didn't get scorched. The power of God was their deliverance. It hid them in the secret place.

But here's what is so exciting. That secret place isn't reserved just for Shadrach, Meshach and Abednego. It isn't reserved only for people who lived thousands of years ago when the Bible was being written.

No! God says anyone who abides in Him can dwell in that secret place. It's for anyone who has the faith to say, "In the secret place of His tent will God hide me; He will set me high upon a rock." It's for anyone who can say like these three Israelites did, "You don't have to worry about us, king. Our God is able to deliver us, and what's more, He will!"

Do you understand that God is not limited? He can do anything it takes to make you safe. He can cover you with His presence in the midst of chemical warfare, nuclear warfare or anything else the devil can come up with. He can bring you through without a scratch.

The only thing that will limit God in your life is unbelief and fear. So determine now to believe God's Word and trust in Him for your safety and protection. You might think, *Yes, Gloria, that's easy for you to say. You don't live in the neighborhood I do.*

Listen, your neighborhood might be bad—but it's still not as bad as Shadrach, Meshach and Abednego's neighborhood. No one is trying to put you into a fiery furnace. And even if they did, God has already proven He can get you out!

CHAPTER 8

FACING THE LIONS

"You shall tread upon the lion and the adder; the young lion and the serpent shall you trample underfoot."

(Psalm 91:13, *AMPC*)

Daniel is a good example of someone who stayed ready. And because he did, the plans his enemies devised for his death failed miserably. Daniel was a contemporary of Shadrach, Meshach and Abednego. He was a member of the royal staff of Babylon just as they were. In fact, Daniel was one of three presidents of the empire, second only to the king himself.

Daniel had so much influence that other presidents and princes became jealous of his position and began looking for ways to get him removed. But the Bible says no matter how hard they looked, "they could find none occasion nor fault; forasmuch as he was faithful." (See Daniel 6:4.)

Daniel was faithful. He was faithful in his service to the king and faithful to God. Finally, the officials who were trying to get Daniel fired realized the only way they were ever going to get him was to put him in a corner by forcing him to choose between God and the king.

So that's what they did. They suggested the king pass a law that forbade anyone from making petition (praying) to anyone other than the king himself for 30 days. Anyone who broke the law would be thrown into a den of lions.

Their suggestion appealed to the king's ego so much that he signed the law on the spot, without even thinking what it would mean to his trusted administrator Daniel. "Now when Daniel knew that the writing was signed, he went into his house; and his windows being open in his chamber toward Jerusalem, he kneeled upon his knees three times a day, and prayed, and gave thanks before his God, as he did aforetime" (verse 10).

Daniel knew about the king's new law. But he wouldn't compromise. He didn't even choose to switch to silent prayer. He simply kept praying just the way he always had.

When the others reported to the king what Daniel had done, the king was grieved. He trusted Daniel and respected him. He didn't want to throw him to the lions but he had been tricked by his staff. He had trapped himself by his own decree and couldn't change it. So, "the king commanded, and Daniel was brought and cast into the den of lions. The king said to Daniel, May your God, Whom you are serving continually, deliver you!" (See verse 16, *AMPC*.)

Notice the king said Daniel served God continually. Remember what we learned about abiding? It meant to dwell continually in a place. Daniel was an abider! He was faithful.

He stayed constantly in the presence and service of God. That was his ongoing state of mind, his natural habitat.

Let's look at what happened to this abider:

And a stone was brought and laid upon the mouth of the den, and the king sealed it with his own signet.... Then the king went to his palace and passed the night fasting, neither were instruments of music or dancing girls brought before him; and his sleep fled from him. Then the king arose very early in the morning and went in haste to the den of lions. And when he came to the den and to Daniel, he cried out in a voice of anguish.... O Daniel, servant of the living God, is your God, Whom you serve continually, able to deliver you from the lions? Then Daniel said to the king, O king, live forever! My God has sent His angel and has shut the lions' mouths so that they have not hurt me.... Then the king was exceedingly glad and commanded that Daniel should be taken up out of the den...and no hurt of any kind was found on him because he believed... in his God (verses 17-23, *AMPC).*

Daniel's deliverance wasn't some kind of one-time thing God did just because He liked Daniel better than most other people. It wasn't just something God did so He'd have an interesting story to put in the Bible. God delivered Daniel because He always delivers those who abide in Him in faith.

You can trust God with your life. He'll do the same thing for you He did for Daniel if—I said if—you abide in Him in faith...trusting, expecting and confessing His delivering power.

SUPERNATURAL TROUBLESHOOTERS

Some people seem to think angels aren't around much anymore. But they are! They were present throughout the Old Testament—and they haven't gone on vacation since then. If you want a New Testament example of their activities, read Acts 12. It tells of a very dangerous time in the history of the early Church. Peter had been arrested:

> Peter therefore was kept in prison: but prayer was made without ceasing of the church unto God for him. And when Herod would have brought him forth, the same night Peter was sleeping between two soldiers, bound with two chains: and the keepers before the door kept the prison (verses 5-6).

It sounds like Peter was in a maximum security situation, doesn't it? In the natural,

there was no possibility of escape. But God's
people were praying and believing God for his
protection—

> And, behold, the angel of the Lord came
> upon him, and a light shined in the prison:
> and he smote Peter on the side, and raised
> him up, saying, Arise up quickly. And his
> chains fell off from his hands (verse 7).

That's the wonderful thing about God's protection. You could hire a hundred natural men
to protect you, but they'd be limited by natural
things. When you're dealing with angels, you're
dealing with the supernatural. That angel didn't
have to have a key made. When he showed
up, the chains that bound Peter just fell off. (If
you'll read the rest of the chapter, you'll find it
was easier for Peter to get out of prison than to
get into the prayer meeting!)

I want you to notice something else about
this situation. Peter wasn't staying up moaning

and groaning about being executed. He was sound asleep. In fact, he was sleeping so soundly the angel had to hit him to wake him up:

> And the angel said unto him, Gird thyself, and bind on thy sandals. And so he did. And he saith unto him, Cast thy garment about thee, and follow me. And he went out, and followed him; and wist not that it was true which was done by the angel; but thought he saw a vision. When they were past the first and second ward, they came unto the iron gate that leadeth unto the city; which opened to them of his own accord: and they went out, and passed on through one street; and forthwith the angel departed from him (verses 8-10).

The angel of God just took Peter out of prison. He had no problems with guards, chains, keys or city gates...he simply woke Peter up, got him out and sent him home.

I could tell you story after story where angels have intervened to drastically alter the outcome of situations, both in the Bible and in our day as well. Some time ago, for example, one of our ministry employees was riding to work on his motorcycle when suddenly a big truck pulled across the road right in front of him. It happened so quickly there was nothing he could do. He didn't have time to think. He didn't have time to speak—he didn't have time to do anything.

Many times that's how things happen. Without warning, suddenly trouble is upon you. It doesn't tell you it's coming in advance so you'll have time to fast and pray. You have to be ready. You have to live every day believing God. You have to say continually, "The Lord is my refuge and my fortress." Because at those moments, you don't have time to say it.

That's how it was with that fellow on the motorcycle. All of a sudden there was a truck in front of him.

That's the last thing he remembered. He saw the truck and everything went blank. The next thing he knew he was walking around on the side of the road. A few yards away, his motorcycle lay underneath the truck.

A girl who was driving right behind him saw the whole thing. She said when the motorcycle slid under the truck, the man who was riding it went up in the air, did a flip and landed safely on his feet by a fence nearby. His only injury was a scratch on the arm.

I can't imagine anything that could make that happen except angels. But here's the point. That fellow was ready. He didn't have time to grab his Bible and brush up on the 91st Psalm. He was already prepared.

That's how it has to be. You can't wait until the last minute and start memorizing scripture when disaster strikes. You need to "say of the Lord" now. You need to stay ready.

CHAPTER 9

THE INWARD WITNESS

"Because he has set his love upon Me, therefore will I deliver him; I will set him on high, because he knows and understands My name [has a personal knowledge of My mercy, love, and kindness—trusts and relies on Me, knowing I will never forsake him, no, never]. He shall call upon Me, and I will answer him; I will be with him in trouble, I will deliver him and honor him. With long life will I satisfy him and show him My salvation."

(Psalm 91:14-16, *AMPC*)

Once you start operating in faith, trusting God to protect and defend you in every situation, something will start happening to you— something you may never have perceived before.

You'll begin hearing some directions from the Holy Spirit.

Sometimes those directions won't seem very spiritual. For example, you may be heading out the door to go grocery shopping, and suddenly, from inside you will come the thought, *Don't go to the store the way you usually go, take a different route. Go this way.* Or, *Don't go to that store, go to another one.*

Why would God say something like that? Maybe because He knows the store you usually go to is about to be robbed, and you would be in danger if you went there. That thought, impression or prompting is the inward witness. It is the Holy Spirit speaking to your spirit for your protection.

There was a devastating earthquake that struck San Francisco in 1990. A close friend of mine, Billye Brim, told me about a friend of hers whose son was working there the day the earthquake hit.

That afternoon he was in his office, as usual, when the thought came to him that he should leave the office early and head for his home in Oakland. The World Series was being played in a stadium nearby and he didn't want to be caught in the traffic on the freeway when the game ended. It just seemed like a natural thought.

He yielded to that impression and left work early that day. If he hadn't, he would have been on that freeway when it collapsed during the earthquake.

The Bible says God speaks in a still, small voice. He doesn't shout directions at you. He gives you impressions, thoughts, promptings and gentle urgings. You have to learn to be sensitive to them.

You also need to be pliable and ready to change your plans when something comes to you from your spirit that seems good. It just might save your life.

How do you become aware of that inward witness? It doesn't happen automatically. It comes by spending time with God. It comes when you listen for it in faith, expecting God to guide you.

You must learn to listen. God may tell you not to take your normal route home in order to save you from a traffic accident or He may tell you not to get on a plane you're scheduled to take. I've heard of several incidents when someone received a distinct impression not to get on an airplane and, sure enough, it crashed. But then again, I've had that thought before I boarded a plane and perceived it was just a natural thought. When you endeavor to follow God moment by moment, day by day, you'll know the difference.

While we are on the subject, Ken and I pray over every plane we ride. As we walk toward the plane we say, "We take authority over this plane in the Name of Jesus. Satan, we bind your power in the Name of Jesus. You'll not touch the equipment, crew or passengers in any way. Ministering spirits (angels) you go before us and clear our way in Jesus' Name."

Usually I'll pray a day or two ahead for the Lord to prepare the crew, equipment and passengers for us, and believe for a hassle-free trip with no delays or bad weather.

No matter how simple the instruction from God may be, pay attention to it. Be quick to listen. The Holy Spirit's job is to warn you of things to come and to minister grace and favor to you every day. Learn to listen to Him!

IT'S GOING TO TAKE TIME

I don't want to scare you, but I do want you to be aware that in the days ahead, you're going to see a great deal of trouble in the world around you. Things on this earth are going to get worse, just like they did in Noah's day. The darkness will get darker and the light will get brighter.

Jesus Himself compared this end-time age to that generation. He said:

> But as the days of Noe were, so shall also the coming of the Son of man be. For as in the days that were before the flood they were eating and drinking, marrying and giving in marriage, until the day that Noe entered into the ark, and knew not until the flood came, and took them all away (Matthew 24:37-39).

There's something we need to learn from Noah. Don't wait until trouble hits to start building your ark. You want to have it finished before trouble comes.

It took Noah many, many years to build his ark. Think about that! There he was, out in the middle of nowhere, building this big ship with no water in sight. Don't you know his neighbors laughed at him? After all, they had never even seen rain.

"Crazy old Noah!" they must have said. "Crazy old Noah and his boys talk about God delivering them from the flood that's coming. They don't know what they're talking about!"

You know, people made fun of Noah and his family all those years and the scriptures say they did not know or understand until the day the flood came and swept them away. They were in the dark. But when the flood came, Noah wasn't in the dark—he was in the ark! He knew exactly what God was going to do and he was prepared.

Today, I am saying to you the same thing God said to Noah. "There's a flood coming. Build yourself an ark!" Build it with the 91st Psalm. Build it with scriptures about your deliverance. Build it by abiding in Almighty God. Build it by saying with your mouth, "I will say of the Lord, He is my refuge and my fortress: my God; in Him will I trust."

Don't wait until the flood comes and sweeps

you away. Start now. Meditate on God's Word of deliverance. Read it. Go over it every day until it is so deeply rooted in your heart that it comes flowing out at the first sign of trouble. Carry this little book around with you until you get so filled with this truth that your heart carries it for you.

Don't be in the dark. Be in the ark. Build yourself an ark—today!

Prayer for Salvation and Baptism in the Holy Spirit

Heavenly Father, I come to You in the Name of Jesus. Your Word says, "Whosoever shall call on the name of the Lord shall be saved" (Acts 2:21). I am calling on You. I pray and ask Jesus to come into my heart and be Lord over my life according to Romans 10:9-10: "If thou shalt confess with thy mouth the Lord Jesus, and shalt believe in thine heart that God hath raised him from the dead, thou shalt be saved. For with the heart man believeth unto righteousness; and with the mouth confession is made unto salvation." I do that now. I confess that Jesus is Lord, and I believe in my heart that God raised Him from the dead. I repent of sin. I renounce it. I renounce the devil and everything he stands for. Jesus is my Lord.

I am now reborn! I am a Christian—a child of Almighty God! I am saved! You also said in Your Word, "If ye then, being evil, know how to give good gifts unto your children: HOW MUCH MORE shall your heavenly Father give the Holy Spirit to them that ask him?" (Luke 11:13). I'm also asking You to fill me with the Holy Spirit. Holy Spirit, rise up within me as I praise God. I fully expect to speak with other tongues as You give me the utterance (Acts 2:4). In Jesus' Name. Amen!

Begin to praise God for filling you with the Holy Spirit. Speak those words and syllables you receive—not in your own language, but the language given to you by the Holy Spirit. You have to use your own voice. God will not force you to speak. Don't be concerned with how it sounds. It is a heavenly language!

Continue with the blessing God has given you and pray in the spirit every day.

You are a born-again, Spirit-filled believer. You'll never be the same!

Find a good church that boldly preaches God's Word and obeys it. Become part of a church family who will love and care for you as you love and care for them.

We need to be connected to each other. It increases our strength in God. It's God's plan for us.

Make it a habit to watch the *Believer's Voice of Victory* broadcast and VICTORY Channel® and become a doer of the Word, who is blessed in his doing (James 1:22-25).

About the Author

Gloria Copeland is a noted author and minister of the gospel whose teaching ministry is known throughout the world. Believers worldwide know her through Believers' Conventions, Victory Campaigns, magazine articles, teaching audios and videos, and the daily and Sunday *Believer's Voice of Victory* television broadcast, which she hosts with her husband, Kenneth Copeland. She is known for Healing School, which she began teaching and hosting in 1979 at KCM meetings. Gloria delivers the Word of God and the keys to victorious Christian living to millions of people every year.

Gloria is author of the New York Times bestseller, *God's Master Plan for Your Life* and *Live Long, Finish Strong,* as well as numerous other favorites, including *God's Will for You, Walk With God, God's Will Is Prosperity, Hidden Treasures* and *To Know Him.* She has also co-authored several books with her husband, including *Family Promises, Healing Promises* and the best-selling daily devotionals, *From Faith to Faith* and *Pursuit of His Presence.*

She holds an honorary doctorate from Oral Roberts University. In 1994, Gloria was voted Christian Woman of the Year, an honor conferred on women whose example demonstrates outstanding Christian leadership. Gloria is also the co-founder and vice president of Kenneth Copeland Ministries in Fort Worth, Texas.

Materials to Help You Receive Your Healing
by Gloria Copeland

Books

* And Jesus Healed Them All
   Don't Buy the Lie
* God's Prescription for Divine Health
* God's Will for Your Healing
* Harvest of Health
   Live Healed
   Three Steps to the Good Life
   Words That Heal (gift book with CD enclosed)

Audio Resources

Be Made Whole—Live Long, Live Healthy
God Wants You Well
Healing Confessions (CD and minibook)
Healing School
How to Get Well, Stay Well, and Enjoy Life

DVD Resources

Be Made Whole—Live Long, Live Healthy
How to Get Well, Stay Well, and Enjoy Life
Know Him As Healer

*Available in Spanish

BELIEVER'S VOICE OF VICTORY

When The LORD first spoke to Kenneth and Gloria Copeland about starting the *Believer's Voice of Victory* magazine...

He said: *This is your seed. Give it to everyone who ever responds to your ministry, and don't ever allow anyone to pay for a subscription!*

For more than 50 years, it has been the joy of Kenneth Copeland Ministries to bring the good news to believers. Readers enjoy teaching from ministers who write from lives of living contact with God, and testimonies from believers experiencing victory through God's Word in their everyday lives.

Today, the *BVOV* magazine is mailed monthly, bringing encouragement and blessing to believers around the world. Many even use it as a ministry tool, passing it on to others who desire to know Jesus and grow in their faith!

Request your FREE subscription to the *Believer's Voice of Victory* magazine today!

Go to **freevictory.com** to subscribe online, or call us **1-800-600-7395** (U.S. only) or **+1-817-852-6000**.

We're Here for You!®

Your growth in God's Word and victory in Jesus are at the very center of our hearts. In every way God has equipped us, we will help you deal with the issues facing you, so you can be the **victorious overcomer** He has planned for you to be.

The mission of Kenneth Copeland Ministries is about all of us growing and going together. Our prayer is that you will take full advantage of all the Lord has given us to share with you.

Wherever you are in the world, you can watch the *Believer's Voice of Victory* broadcast on television (check your local listings), kcm.org and digital streaming devices like Roku®. You can also watch the broadcast as well as programs from dozens of ministers you can trust on our 24/7 faith network—Victory Channel®. Visit govictory.com for show listings and all the ways to watch.

Our website, **kcm.org,** gives you access to every resource we've developed for your victory. And, you can find contact information for our international offices in Africa, Australia, Canada, Europe, Ukraine, Latin America and our headquarters in the United States.

Each office is staffed with devoted men and women, ready to serve and pray with you. You can contact the worldwide office nearest you for assistance, and you can call us for prayer at our U.S. number, +1-817-852-6000, every day of the week!

We encourage you to connect with us often and let us be part of your everyday walk of faith!

Jesus Is LORD!

Kenneth & Gloria Copeland

Kenneth and Gloria Copeland